HIDDEN TREASURES

AMAZING STORIES

FROM THE

OLD TESTAMENT

BROADMAN
&HOLMAN
PUBLISHERS

NASHVILLE, TENNESSEE

For Matthew
Jeremiah 29:11

Library of Congress Cataloging-in-Publication Data

Simon, Mary Manz, 1948-
    Hidden treasures : amazing stories from the Old Testament / by Mary Manz Simon ;
illustrations by Jeff Preston.
        p. cm.
    ISBN 0-8054-2328-1
1. Bible stories, English--O.T. [1. Bible stories--O.T.] I. Preston, Jeff, 1958-, ill. II.
Title.

    BS551.2 .S545 2000
    221.9'505--dc21

                                                                                    00-037910

1 2 3 4 5   04 03 02 01 00

TABLE OF CONTENTS

A Narrow Escape 1

Showdown at the Well 5

The Jealous King 9

Deborah Wins a War 13

The Secret of the Arrow 17

The Poison Pot of Stew 21

The Pharaoh's Cruel Order 25

Abigail's Gifts 29

The Voice in the Cave 33

The Battle Won with a Song 37

A Narrow Escape

The spies crouched low. Creeping silently, they edged along the city wall. They hid in the lengthening shadows as the sun started to slip behind the horizon. The spies needed to get inside the city gates before Jericho was closed for the night. Scrambling quickly, they scooted through the gates, hoping they wouldn't be seen. The men were on a secret mission for Joshua, the leader of God's people. They were to learn about the city of Jericho and report back to Joshua. Now inside the city, they hunkered down next to the city wall. "Did anybody see us?" whispered the younger spy.

"I don't know," his friend whispered back. "We've got to find a safe place to hide."

"Someone will see us if we cross the street," the younger spy observed. "We should look for a room built into the city wall."

"You learn quickly, my young friend," murmured the older spy, nodding his approval. Signaling with his hand, he urged his companion to move ahead. They finally came to the home of a woman named Rahab, whose house was built into the thick city wall. Breathing a sigh of relief, the spies began to relax as Rahab led them to a hiding place.

They didn't know that someone had seen them sneak inside. At that very moment, men were warning the king of Jericho that spies were in the city. Soldiers headed for the home of Rahab. Soon they pounded on her door.

"Where are the spies?" demanded the king's soldier.

"Do you want a clue?" Rahab asked.

"Where are the spies?" the soldier demanded again.

"Why don't you look just outside the city?" Rahab suggested. "If you hurry, you might still get out of the gates before they are locked, and catch the spies yet tonight."

Grateful for the tip, the soldiers left quickly. When the men were out of sight, Rahab climbed the steps to her roof. She had hidden the spies there beneath plants that were drying.

Rahab peeled back the stalks and motioned it was safe to come out. Even before he emerged from his hiding place, the younger spy asked, "Why did you protect us?"

As Rahab helped the men brush off the strands of flax that clung to their clothes she said, "I know you are God's people. We have heard of the many ways God has helped you.

We know God is with you."

The older spy asked, "We are here to learn everything about your city."

Rahab answered, "The people of Jericho are afraid of you because they know God is with you. That's why the king sent his soldiers to find you."

The spies looked at each other. Rahab was giving them valuable information to share with Joshua. Rahab continued, "Because God is with you, we know you will win any battle."

The spies listened intently: Joshua needed to know that, because the people of Jericho were so afraid, it would be easy to enter the city.

"We must tell Joshua," said the older spy. "But how can we get out of the city?" asked his companion. "The gates are locked for the night."

"Come with me," said Rahab. Going downstairs, she looked through her things. Discarding one item after another, she finally found a long piece of rope. Tugging to check its strength, she knew it would work for what she had planned.

"I will lower you through the window," Rahab said. "But you must promise that when you and the rest of God's people come to Jericho, you will protect my family."

The men nodded. "We are grateful for your help tonight," the older spy said. "Hang a red cord outside your window when we leave, and everyone in your house will be safe."

Rahab smiled her thanks, and the three of them moved toward a window that opened directly outside the city wall. If the spies could escape through the window and then hide, they would be safe.

Carefully, Rahab lowered the heavy rope. First one, then the other spy held on tightly. Hand-over-hand they slid down the lifeline. When the second spy reached the ground, Rahab pulled up the rope. Then she flung the red cord out the window.

When Joshua and God's people finally entered the city, Rahab and all in her family were saved. She had helped God's people, and they had kept their promise to her.

Based on Joshua 2

To Talk About:

1. Why did Rahab protect the spies?

2. What would you have told the soldiers who knocked at the door?

3. Did Rahab have courage? Talk about what courage means.

Showdown at the Well

Moses reached down to loosen his sandal. He had walked for so many days, the strap had rubbed a blister on his heel. He eased his body against the wall at the well.

"Ah," Moses sighed gratefully as he untied the sandal strap. "That feels so much better," he murmured.

Moses appreciated these moments of rest. He reached forward and laid his head on his arms. His whole body ached with tiredness. Moses had never traveled so far. He longed to sleep. Even the sound of distant voices couldn't keep him from a needed rest.

Moses barely stirred as the voices came closer. Without even lifting his head, he knew that others had come to the well.

"I want to wash off this cut on the lamb's leg before we draw water for the flock," one woman said.

"I'm just glad we found the little thing," said another shepherdess.

Moses could hear the soft bleating of the lamb as the women calmed the animal.

Moses felt so relaxed, he didn't even want to open his eyes. Now Moses could sense others were coming to draw water.

The women seemed happy as they talked quietly with each other.

"Filling troughs for the whole flock could take a long time," he thought tiredly. "It's good they like their work."

Moses was almost lulled to sleep by the slow and steady movements of the women. But suddenly, he was jolted awake. He glanced up just in time to see several other shepherds push the women away from the well. "Get away from here," one man said roughly. Another shepherd raised his staff as a weapon, and the women scattered in fear. The men clustered around the well and rapidly began to draw water.

Moses reached down to tighten his sandal. Then he stood up.

"The women were here first," he said.

The men at the well looked up, then hesitated for a moment. Moses lifted his staff, as if he would strike the nearest man. The shepherd dumped the jar in disgust, and the others motioned him away.

"Aw, we'll come back later," he grumbled. The unhappy shepherd joined the other men who led their flocks to nearby hills.

Moses said nothing. He merely turned and gestured to the women. They could return, he waved. The women hesitated. They came back cautiously, still afraid that danger was lurking.

"Those men won't hurt you now," Moses assured them. "Here, let me help you." Moses began filling the jars almost as quickly as the women could empty the water into the sheep troughs.

Working together, the job was soon finished.

After thanking Moses, the women returned home. Moses limped back to the wall near the well, grateful to loosen the sandal once more. His heel was still sore. He needed to rest before traveling again.

Moses had just settled into a comfortable position when he heard voices again. He looked up to see two of the women hurrying toward him.

"Come," a shepherdess said. "Our father would like you to join us for supper. He would like to express his gratitude for your help."

Moses looked up with tired eyes. A home-cooked meal and pleasant conversation might be just what he needed.

Once again, he tied his sandal. As he reached for his staff, Moses smiled gratefully.

"Now it is my turn to say 'Thank you,'" he said.

Based on
Exodus 2: 15-21

To Talk About:

1. Moses had traveled a long distance. What is the longest trip you've taken?

2. Moses helped people he didn't know. Has your family ever helped someone even if you didn't know them?

3. The words 'Thank you' are important. Think back for a moment. When did you last say 'Thank you?'

The Jealous King

We won," the people shouted. "We won!"

"Long live David," they said. "Long live David, the warrior!"

King Saul looked down into the streets to see what all the cheering was about. He muttered to himself, "Those people are cheering David again.

I want them to cheer me," he said. A deep frown settled in his brow. He fingered his sword nervously. Outside the crowds grew larger. The shouts grew louder.

"Long live David, the great warrior," the people said again and again.

King Saul saw David wave and smile at the people. God had watched over David and the soldiers. With God's help, they had won another great battle.

Slowly David made his way through the crowd. He was eager to report to the palace. He was sure King Saul would be pleased with their victory.

David prepared to meet the king. He unfastened the heavy armor. He set aside the shield and propped his long spear against the wall. Then the mighty warrior reached for his harp. David strummed softly to check the tuning.

King Saul loved David's music. After today's victory, David thought the songs would sound especially sweet.

David bowed low before the throne, then reported, "My king, God was with our army. We have won another great battle."

"Yes," said Saul, fingering the spear at his side. "The people are cheering for you again."

"God was with us," David repeated. He glanced at the frowning Saul seated above him. David was puzzled. Why wasn't the king celebrating?

David did not say anything else. Instead, he reached for his harp. Soft music would certainly please his king. David strummed softly. Gently, the soothing music floated through the air.

"King Saul," David started to say, but the king jumped up with an angry shout. Clutching his spear he pulled back his arm. Aiming directly at David, King Saul flung the spear with a mighty shout.

"The people should cheer me," raged the angry ruler.

The spear ripped David's cloak with a jagged tear as he dashed from the room.

David raced out the palace doors and tore through the streets. Breathing heavily, he finally rushed through the door to his home.

"Michal," panted David. "King Saul tried to kill me."

Michal looked at her husband's torn clothing. Fear was frozen onto his sweaty face. Clank, clank, clank. The noise of the king's messengers marching toward the house startled them.

"You must escape," Michal said.

Frantic, she raced to a back window. Michal lowered a rope and David slid down. With a quick wave to his wife, David escaped.

Rap, rap, rap came the knock at the door. The king's messengers had already come for David.

Michal thought quickly. Her husband needed time to get farther away. Michal needed to stall the

11

king's men. She glanced around the room. She dragged an old statue to the bed. Then she threw on an old prayer shawl, a long belt, and some clothes. Rap, rap, rap came the insistent knock at the door.

Michal smoothed the clothes so it looked like a person in bed. Then she laid a sheet over the top. At the last moment, she flung on some goat hair at the top.

"There," she paused briefly. "It almost looks like a person in bed."

Rap, rap, rap, the knocking came again. "The king's messengers command you to open this door." Michal straightened her clothes, then walked calmly to the door.

"Yes?" she asked sweetly.

"Where is David?" growled a messenger.

"My husband is not seeing visitors right now," Michal explained and firmly closed the door.

Rap, rap, rap the knocking started again. Once again, Michal greeted the messengers with a smile. "Yes?" Michal asked.

"King Saul wants to see David," one of the men explained, pushing his way inside. "Take us to him."

Michal slowly led the messengers upstairs. Putting her finger to her lips and tiptoeing, she pointed silently to the bed.

One of the messengers stepped closer. He stared at the figure. He went up to the edge of the bed. The stuffed clothing looked almost like a person, but the goat's hair did not look like David's hair!

"Who is sleeping in this bed?" the messenger demanded. Michal said nothing, as the king's men ripped apart the sheets. The statue stared back. The messengers had been tricked.

By now, David was far away.

Based on 1 Samuel 19:8-16

To Talk About:

1. When do you think David was most afraid? Talk about a time you have been in a scary situation.

2. God gave Michal the gift of a creative mind. What talents has God given you?

3. How do you think King Saul reacted when he heard that David had escaped?

12

Deborah Wins a War

Deborah looked up. A gentle breeze rustled the palm leaves above her. *How often I've been grateful for the shade of this tree,* she thought.

Years ago, as a little girl, Deborah crawled under the leaves of "her" baby tree. The branches bent to the ground, and Deborah was completely hidden. Deborah smiled, remembering how much she loved her secret hideaway. Camels glided by. Travelers passed. Older boys chased around, and nobody even knew she was there. Deborah shivered a bit, though, as she remembered one horrible day when a group of the king's soldiers had chased some of God's people right past her tree. But that day, as always, she stayed hidden under the branches.

Through the years, her hideaway was a perfect place to pray. Deborah's prayer was always the same: God, deliver our people from these cruel masters.

Deborah and "her" tree both grew up. Even though Deborah grew taller, the tree grew faster. Soon, Deborah could barely touch the top branches. And by the time Deborah became a young woman, the tree towered above her. But during all these years, Deborah continued to pray under "her" tree. And her prayer was always the same: God, deliver our people from these cruel masters.

Deborah got married. She ran a household, and yet everyone still knew about Deborah and the palm tree.

"Looking for Deborah?" people would ask.

"She's under her tree," others would answer. For Deborah still spent hours praying to God, leaning against the trunk of the tall tree. Deborah asked God for wisdom, so she could help her people as they struggled to live under a cruel king and his army commander, Sisera. And God blessed her.

Day after day, people came to wise Deborah. When people had questions they couldn't answer, they came to Deborah. When people had arguments, Deborah solved their problems under her palm tree.

One day, Deborah called Barak to the palm tree. Deborah said, "I have a message for you from the Lord. You are to gather ten thousand men at Mt. Tabor. The Lord will trick the cruel army commander Sisera into coming out to fight you. And then, Barak, the Lord will help you defeat the army!"

Barak was shocked. He couldn't fight Sisera. Sisera had 900 iron chariots. Sisera had a trained army. So Barak said to Deborah, "I'm not going unless you go with me."

Deborah thought for a moment. Then she agreed and said, "I will go, but I'm warning you. The Lord will let a woman defeat Sisera, so no one will honor you for winning the battle."

Deborah left the shade of her tree to accompany Barak. He gathered ten thousand men at Mt. Tabor, just as the Lord had commanded.

The evil Sisera had heard about Barak and his men. So Sisera called together the drivers for his 900 iron chariots and his entire army. They set up camp below the mountain.

Deborah and Barak looked down from Mt. Tabor. The iron chariots glistened in the brilliant sun. Sisera and his army were waiting. Barak's heart pounded when he saw what his men faced, but Deborah knew the Lord would keep His promise. She and Barak waited for the battle to begin. Deborah was up early the next morning.

"Barak," she shouted. "Today is the day. It's time to attack Sisera. The Lord will help you win. The Lord has already gone ahead to fight for you."

Barak gathered his troops. The men began to stream down the mountain. But as they moved closer to the camps of Sisera, God sent a terrible storm in front of them. The skies darkened. Rain began to pour down. The winds blew, pelting Sisera's troops with stinging rain. The chariot drivers urged their animals forward, but instead, the animals stampeded. Sisera's troops were confused. They had nowhere to turn. Soon everyone and everything was stuck in the mud.

Barak's men quickly attacked. Sisera's troops were completely wiped out. The Lord's army had won a great victory. Even Sisera, who escaped from the battlefield, was later killed by a brave woman, just as Deborah had said would happen.

Deborah and Barak called everyone together to celebrate. They thanked God with long and happy songs. They danced with shouts of joy. Again and again the people sang the story of how God had delivered them. And God's people enjoyed peace for forty years.

Based on
Judges 4: 3-16

To Talk About:

1. Deborah liked to think under a tree. Where do you go when you like to think?

2. We often think of soldiers winning a battle. But how did Deborah, who wasn't a soldier, help Barak win a battle?

3. Who was the braver person: Deborah or Barak?

The Secret of the Arrow

"What have I done wrong?" David mumbled to himself. A frown lined his forehead as he searched for an answer.

David was the bravest warrior in the land. He had killed the giant, Goliath. He had led King Saul's people to great victories. After each battle, grateful people had filled the streets cheering "David, David, David!" That's why he was so puzzled.

"Why does King Saul want to kill me?" David wondered aloud. David asked his best friend, the crown prince Jonathan, the same question.

"Why does your father want to kill me?" David asked. "He threw his spear at me in the palace."

"You are the bravest warrior in the land," said Jonathan. "You killed the giant, Goliath. You have led our people to great victories."

David nodded, but added, "I don't feel safe. Your father still wants to kill me." Although Jonathan tried to comfort his friend, David was convinced he was in danger. Jonathan didn't like to see his friend upset, so he offered to talk with his father at dinner.

"I am sure you are safe," Jonathan repeated. "And besides, my father never does anything without talking with me."

David listened, but was not reassured. He said, "Just to be sure I'm safe, I

am going to hide until you talk with your father. Where can we meet?"

The friends put together a plan with a secret signal. In the morning, Jonathan would take his bow and arrow out to the fields for target practice. Only David and Jonathan would know the secret signal: if Jonathan told his servant, "The arrow is right by you," then David would be safe. If Jonathan told his servant, "The arrow is beyond you," then David would be in danger.

David liked the plan. He could hide in the hills, and no one would be suspicious of Jonathan practicing with his bow and arrow.

Jonathan added, "Even if my father has spies searching for you, no one will know that the words are a secret signal."

Then David went into hiding and Jonathan returned to the palace.

The next morning, just as they had planned, Jonathan gathered his bow and arrows. He and his servant walked to the field for target practice. The prince told his servant, "I'm going to practice shooting this morning. Stand aside, then find the arrows for me."

Jonathan threaded an arrow. Aiming carefully for a specific target, he pulled back on the bow. The arrow sailed through the sky. Again and again Jonathan arched arrows through the sky. Racing to gather the arrows as they fell, the servant criss-crossed the field.

Finally Jonathan called loudly to his servant, "Oh look, the arrow is beyond you."

Once again, the servant bent to retrieve an arrow, not knowing Jonathan had just given David a secret signal.

"Hurry now, go back to the city," Jonathan told his servant, as he filled the quiver. When Jonathan stood alone on the field, David edged out from his hiding place. His face was sad, for the secret message had indicated King Saul still wanted to hurt him.

As he watched his friend approach, tears ran down Jonathan's cheeks. He had tried his best for his friend. He had reminded his father of David's heroic actions on battlefields. He had told his father of David's loyal service.

But King Saul had not listened. David had been right: his life was in danger. Now Jonathan knew he would need to say goodbye to his best friend.

David and Jonathan talked about the times they had shared. They talked about their promise to care for each other's families. And they cried together, overcome with sadness.

Finally Jonathan stood and said to David, "Go in peace. May the Lord be with you."

Jonathan walked back to the city. And David left the field, to search for a safe place.

Based on
1 Samuel 20

To Talk About:

1. David and Jonathan were best friends. What does it mean to be a best friend?

2. Jonathan was loyal to David. That means Jonathan stood up for his friend, even when it was hard. When have you been a loyal friend?

3. Can you think of a time when it would not be good to be loyal to a friend?

The Poison Pot of Stew

Grrrrr

The young student glanced up with an embarrassed look. Had anyone heard his stomach growl?

Grrrrr

The sons of the prophets loved learning from Elisha, but right now, one student had a problem: he was starved. It wasn't lunchtime yet, but he was hungry.

And he wasn't the only one. A famine had hit the country. People everywhere were hungry most of the time. There just wasn't enough food.

Grrrrr

This time, Elisha looked up with an amused smile.

"I think someone is telling me that it's time to eat," said God's prophet. "It's hard to learn on an empty stomach, so we'll continue the lesson after lunch."

Elisha stood and stretched. He had been teaching all morning. Even he was ready for some food.

"Put on the large pot," Elisha directed. "Let's boil some stew."

Elisha watched as the students trekked to nearby fields. He knew the young men would need to look hard to find any leftover vegetables. Many people were going hungry during the famine. Most fields had been

stripped bare, with only a few weeds lying limply on the ground.

"Peas," called one student, happily stripping a plant. A shout of joy from a distant field meant another success.

"Onions" yelled another, as he scrounged in the dry soil for the tiny bulbs. The students drifted farther and farther away: no one wanted to return to Elisha empty-handed.

Water was boiling in the large pot as the students drifted back with various offerings. One brought a couple of strange-looking vegetables he had found underneath some leaves. Another brought some gourds which he had found hanging limply on a vine.

"What are those?" asked a student.

Looking at the unfamiliar gourds, the student shrugged.

"I don't know," he admitted. "But I couldn't find anything else."

"Are those safe to eat?" asked another.

"I don't know," he admitted again. But everyone was so hungry, no one asked any more questions. The unusual gourds were chopped up with the other vegetables and tossed into the stew pot.

A faint smell of something cooking began to drift from the fire.

"I can't wait for a good meal," said one of the students eagerly. The young men gathered around the pot, anxious to be served. But as the young men took their first bites, one called out to Elisha, "Oh, master! The stew tastes poisonous."

"Stop eating," yelled another.

"It's those odd gourds," said one of the students. "We didn't know what they were, but we needed more food."

Some of the students nodded in agreement. During the famine when people were desperate, many of them had eaten strange or unfamiliar foods. Expecting Elisha to solve the problem, they gathered around the steaming pot.

Elisha said, "Bring me some flour."

Looking into the bubbling brew, Elisha tossed the flour into the stew. Then he said, "You may serve this now."

The students re-filled their bowls with the new stew: there was nothing harmful left in the pot. So they had a good meal, and were grateful that God worked a miracle through His prophet and their teacher, Elisha.

Based on
2 Kings 4: 38-41

To Talk About:

1. How did Elisha help his students?

2. Can you think of a time when you were in trouble and God helped you?

3. Who has taught you about God's Word? Thank God for His gift of a good teacher.

The Pharaoh's Cruel Order

"Waah. Waah."

The first wail of a newborn baby filled the air. People in nearby rooms cheered. Joyful shouts filled the air. Friends and relatives began to praise God. Gratefully, the new parents turned to thank the nurses, Shiphrah and Puah. The women had stayed through the long night to be sure the birth went smoothly. Collecting their things, the nurses tiredly walked home. Although they had helped many women give birth, the nurses still marveled at the miracle of every new life.

"Did you see those perfect little fingers?" asked Shiphrah.

"And did you watch that tiny little mouth open for a yawn?" Puah asked.

"God is truly great," said Shiphrah.

"Oh yes," nodded Puah. "Every time a child is born, I thank God from the bottom of my heart."

"We have the most wonderful job in the world," said Shiphrah. Her friend nodded sadly. There was little joy among the Hebrew people during these years. The cruel Egyptian Pharaoh made God's people work as slaves. Day after day the slaves pounded mud into bricks. The slaves worked furiously to build taller buildings and sculpt finer statues. They worked faster in the fields to harvest more grain. But the Egyptians never

rewarded the Israelites. Instead, the slave masters worked God's people harder than ever. The birth of a baby was one of the few times the Israelites could celebrate.

Now nearing their homes, the women were so intent on thanking God for the gift of a healthy child, that they didn't see their path was blocked. Two of Pharaoh's soldiers were planted in the center of the road.

"Halt," a soldier said gruffly. Startled, the women looked up.

"Pharaoh wants to see you," said the other guard.

"We are nurses," trembled Shiphrah. "We have done nothing wrong."

"We have just delivered another child," explained Puah. "We are only doing our work."

"Come," said the soldier, roughly reaching to grab Puah's arm. "Pharaoh is waiting."

Stumbling under the armed guard's grasp, the women were white with fear when they

reached the palace. Pharaoh stared fiercely from his throne. The nurses shrank back, afraid.

"There are too many Hebrew babies," he said. "If a Hebrew woman gives birth to a boy, kill the child."

Stunned and shaken, the women nodded, bowed, and ran from the palace. At a safe distance, they collapsed in tears and exhaustion. What could they do? They loved God. They could not hurt His people. But they were afraid of Pharaoh. If they disobeyed the ruler, they could be killed. Too tired to think, the women continued toward home and fell into a troubled sleep.

Later, the women prayed to God. They knew God was the giver of life.

They would risk their own lives to be faithful to Him.

During the next days, the nurses continued to deliver infants. Each time a baby girl was born, they thanked God for the blessing of a child. Each time a baby boy was born, they thanked God for the blessing of a child.

Although the nurses were afraid of Pharaoh, they could not kill a baby. Soon the soldiers dragged Shiphrah and Puah back to the palace. Once again, the women stood before Pharaoh. The king looked down fiercely from his throne.

This time, Shiphrah and Puah stared right back at the king.

"There are too many Hebrew babies," Pharaoh roared. "Why are you letting the baby boys live?"

God was good to the nurses and gave them the right words to say. Shiphrah looked directly into the cold eyes of Pharaoh and explained, "The Hebrew women have their babies very quickly."

"Yes, and by the time we get there," continued Puah, "the babies are already born."

Pharaoh, who did not understand such things, dismissed the nurses with an angry wave of his hand. Shiphrah and Puah continued to help Hebrew women give birth to their babies. And because the women had so faithfully served God, He blessed each nurse with children of her own.

Based on Exodus 1: 15-21

To Talk About:

1. Talk about when you were born. How long were you? How much did you weigh?

2. Do you agree with the nurses' decision to disobey Pharaoh?

3. Talk about a time you were rewarded for making the right choice.

Abigail's Gifts

Nabal and Abigail were an odd couple.

Nabal was rough and mean. His name meant "fool." Abigail was thoughtful and wise. Her name meant "source of joy." Everyone who knew the odd couple thought their names matched them perfectly.

Nabal, a rich farmer, had one thousand goats and three thousand sheep. While Nabal's shepherds sheared the sheep in the desert, David, the warrior for God's people, was nearby. David's men watched so that no one stole anything. They protected the shepherds and their sheep. Nabal's men felt so safe that they told others, "We feel as if David had built a walled city around our flock."

David was happy to help, even though he had never met the owner of the sheep. That's why one day David was pleased to hear that Nabal was nearby with another flock. This would be an opportunity to meet the man whose shepherds David had protected in the desert. So David sent ten men to Nabal's camp with this friendly greeting: "My friend and brother, we have watched over your shepherds and sheep. Please be so kind and share some food with us."

David's men waited outside for Nabal's reply. David's men had been living in the desert for a long time. They could almost taste the wonderful festival food that would be served during this time of sheep-shearing. But they did not anticipate Nabal's response to David's message. Scowling fiercely, Nabal growled, "I'm not going to share my food and water. Why should I?" Stunned by the insult, David's men quickly left Nabal's camp, hurrying to tell David what happened.

When David heard how rudely his men had been treated, he ordered, "Everyone get your swords." David directed 200 men to stay and guard his camp. He led 400 other men straight across the desert toward Nabal.

Meanwhile, one of Nabal's servants had run to Abigail. The servant told Abigail how her

husband had mis-treated David's men. The servant spoke faster and faster, because danger was coming closer with every moment.

"Please help us," the servant begged Abigail. "Do something. David and his men are coming to kill us because Nabal insulted them."

Abigail paused only a moment. Then she calmly directed her servants, "Gather the donkeys. Load two hundred loaves of bread. Bring two large jugs. Gather one hundred handfuls of raisins. Add two hundred handfuls of figs."

The servants obeyed immediately: they knew their lives depended on Abigail's gifts. One donkey carried a large sack of roasted grain. Fresh meat was tied into other packs. Then Abigail climbed onto the back of a donkey and rode down the path.

Just as she rounded the hillside, she met David leading his 400 men. Abigail quickly slid off her donkey and bowed deeply before him. Apologizing for her husband, she said, "Nabal means 'fool' and his name fits him," she said. "I did not see your messengers, but please, take this food and share it with your men."

Surprised by her words, David looked at the long line of donkeys. Every animal carried a heavy load. He turned back to Abigail just as she began to speak again.

"God has promised to make you the ruler of His people," Abigail said. "God will reward you for protecting innocent people like us."

David was amazed at the wisdom of the woman who stood in front of him. Nodding slowly, he admitted she was right.

"I thank God He sent you to me," David said. "You have saved the lives of many people today."

David graciously stepped forward to accept Abigail's gifts. With a grateful smile, David told her, "You may go home now. You will be safe."

Nabal, the fool, died shortly after this. Later, Abigail married David, and she brought him joy and happiness.

Based on 1 Samuel 25

To Talk About:

1. What does your name mean?

2. Abigail prevented a big problem. When have you prevented trouble?

3. Abigail was a wise woman. What does it mean to be wise?

The Voice in the Cave

His heart was pounding. He gasped for air. Elijah had been running for hours. His legs felt ready to drop off. But Elijah was afraid to stop – even for a moment. Queen Jezebel was after him. She said she would kill him. Elijah had to keep running. "Keep going. Keep going," he whispered to himself. At last he left the city behind. Elijah kept running and running and running toward the wilderness. Finally, he sat down under a tree. *I did my best, but it wasn't good enough*, he thought. *Queen Jezebel has gotten rid of all God's other helpers. I'm the only one left.* "Dear God," he prayed, "I have worked very hard for You. But I don't think I can do any more. Why won't You help me?" Then he closed his eyes and went to sleep.

"Elijah, Elijah. Wake up and eat," whispered a soft voice in his ear. Elijah awoke with a start. He jumped up thinking it was the queen. But an angel stood in front of him. "Get up and eat," the angel said. Elijah sniffed. *I know that smell*, he thought. *Fresh bread – right here in the wilderness.* He turned and saw fresh bread baking on hot stones. A jug of water sat nearby.

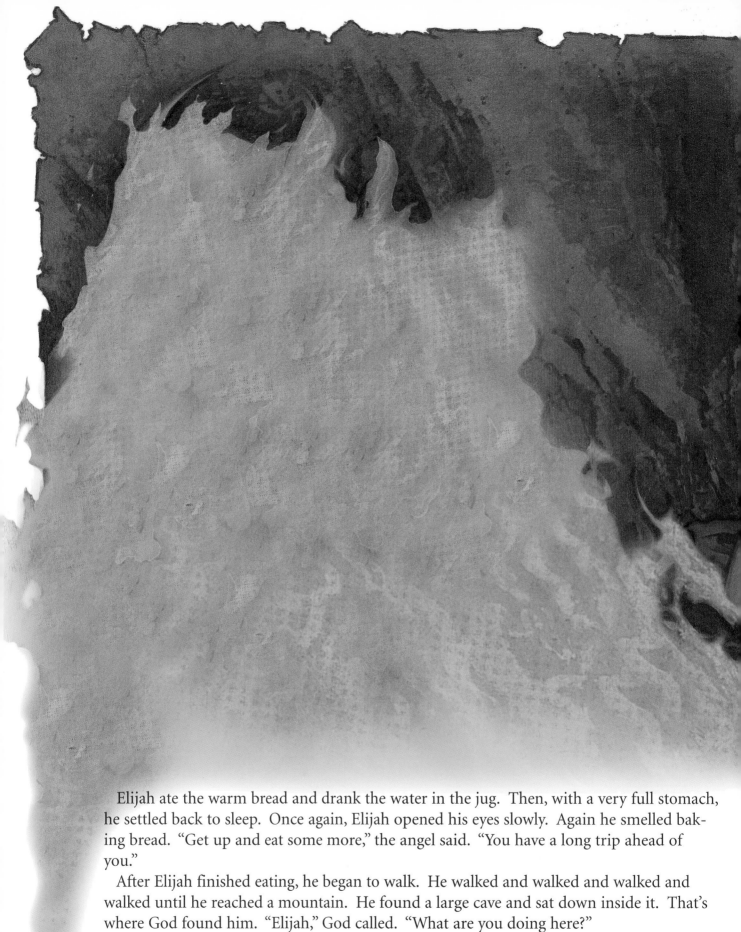

Elijah ate the warm bread and drank the water in the jug. Then, with a very full stomach, he settled back to sleep. Once again, Elijah opened his eyes slowly. Again he smelled baking bread. "Get up and eat some more," the angel said. "You have a long trip ahead of you."

After Elijah finished eating, he began to walk. He walked and walked and walked and walked until he reached a mountain. He found a large cave and sat down inside it. That's where God found him. "Elijah," God called. "What are you doing here?"

"I did my best, God," Elijah said. "But it just wasn't good enough. Queen Jezebel has killed all Your other helpers. Now she wants to kill me, too. Why won't You help me?"

"Leave this cave," God said, "and stand on the mountain." Elijah cautiously stepped

out of the cave. A strong wind began to blow. It whistled and whooshed louder and louder and louder. Rocks tumbled down the mountain around him.

"God, God, where are You?" Elijah called. He looked hard, but he couldn't find God in the wind. Then the earth started to tremble and shake. The shaking grew stronger and stronger and stronger. The whole mountain moved under his feet.

"God, God, are You there?" Elijah called. He looked hard, but he couldn't find God in the earthquake. Then a roaring fire started. It crackled and burned hotter and hotter and hotter. Elijah stumbled back into the cave as the trees and bushes went up in flames. "God, God, I can't see You," Elijah called. He looked hard, but he couldn't find God in the fire. Finally, everything was quiet. Elijah listened. Then, very softly, someone called his name.

"Elijah," the voice whispered.

Elijah peeked out from the cave. "God?"

"Elijah," God said, "why are you here?" Elijah told God about evil Queen Jezebel. He told God how hard he had worked. Elijah told God that he couldn't do any more. He was too tired and lonely. God listened. Then He said, "Follow the desert road. You will find a helper and many people who know about Me. Then you won't be alone."

"Yes, Lord," Elijah said. "I will go."

Elijah walked and walked and walked. His tired legs could barely move, but his heart was jumping for joy. *God will always be here for me*, Elijah thought. *All I have to do is stop talking and start listening.*

Based on
1 Kings 19: 3-16

To Talk About:

1. Elijah ran and ran and ran. Talk about a time someone chased you.

2. Elijah was afraid and lonely, so he talked with God. When you are afraid and lonely, with whom do you talk?

3. Sometimes we describe heroes as brave people. Would you call Elijah a hero? Why?

The Battle Won with a Song

Panting heavily, the messengers dashed toward the palace. Their message was urgent. They rushed to see the king.

Stumbling in their hurry to deliver the news, the messengers almost tripped over their words.

"The armies," panted one. "Three armies...."

"Three armies have captured a city," explained a second messenger.

"They are headed this way," they continued. "Three armies are coming to destroy us."

Lines of worry settled on the face of the king.

King Jehoshaphat had feared an attack. He had a small country. He had a small army. And now enemy soldiers from three powerful armies were almost on his doorstep.

Keeping his head down to hide his fear, the king paced the palace floor. He threw back his robe and commanded, "Have everyone come to the temple now. Bring all the people."

The king and temple helpers were waiting as people gathered in the courtyard of the temple. Children, parents, babies, grandparents, and soldiers crowded close to hear the king's words. But instead of speaking to the people, Jehoshaphat prayed aloud to God. The king knew he could not save the people. The king knew his armies could not save the people. King Jehoshaphat knew only God could save them.

Then one of the temple helpers stepped forward with a message from God.

"Your Majesty," the man said boldly. "Don't be discouraged. Don't be afraid. This battle belongs to the Lord. We will win without a fight!"

The king bowed low to honor God. The temple helpers broke out in loud and joyful songs. "Praise the Lord!" they sang. "Praise the Lord!" And everyone thanked God for the victory that was promised.

The next morning, the king stood before the people again. Before they even left to meet the enemy armies, Jehoshaphat reminded everyone of God's promise. The king's voice boomed out over the crowd. "Don't be discouraged. Don't be afraid. This battle belongs to the Lord. If we believe God's promise to us, we will win without a fight!"

Then Jehoshaphat asked the soldiers to move to the back.

He asked the temple helpers, who had praised God with glorious songs just the day before, to come to the front. Then, with the singers leading the army, they marched toward the battlefield.

"Praise the Lord," sang the people.

"Praise the Lord," they sang, as they marched even closer to the armies.

"Praise the Lord," they sang even louder as they neared the enemy troops.

In the distance, the enemy armies heard the songs. The soldiers were confused. Panic broke out. They began to fight for their lives. The battle raged, as soldiers from the three armies fought among themselves.

"Praise the Lord," God's people sang as they neared the battle site.

The words of their song still hung in the air as King Jehoshaphat marched with the singers, followed by the soldiers, to a lookout above the battle site. The singing stopped as everyone crowded forward to view the scene below. An eerie silence filled the air. Not a single soldier moved on the battlefield. The battle had raged so furiously that no one was left to fight God's people.

God had already won the victory for them!

King Jehoshaphat, the singers, and the soldiers marched back home.

"Praise the Lord," they sang, as they left the site of God's battle. "Praise the Lord," they sang, as they celebrated God's victory. "Praise the Lord," people greeted them, with shouts of joy as they entered the temple. A burst of trumpets and the sound of harps filled the air. God had kept His promise.

He had won the battle without asking the people to fight. And because King Jehoshaphat and the people had believed God's promise, they lived in peace for many, many years.

Based on 2 Chronicles 20

To Talk About:

1. When the king heard that three armies were ready to attack, what did he do first?

2. What is the name of your favorite song in which you praise God?

3. The people of God celebrated with trumpets and harps. What instruments are used in your church?

40